IGNITING THE SPARKS OF THE

By 1632 each settler had his own plot of land on which he ha[...]
settlement spread to the North End, it was apparent that Bos[...]
in the colony and would be the capital of both the colony and[...]
prospered in the next hundred years and in so doing moved a[...]
and all it stood for. Dramatic events such as the Boston Tea Party, the Boston Massacre,
the British advance on Lexington and Concord, and the Battle of Bunker Hill, being part
of Boston and the surrounding areas, were all part of the beginning of the American
Revolution. Boston's great meeting places, Faneuil Hall and the Old South Meeting House,
were the sites of public debates and speeches by American patriots that spurred on these
dramatic events.

THE CIVIL WAR AND CIVIL RIGHTS

The Underground Railroad, using Boston's Beacon Street, became a very important part of the
Civil War. In Boston, by the late 1770s, the Blacks were by and large free, unlike the rest of the
country. Even so they struggled with housing, education and equal pay issues. These issues
were only addressed 150 years later by the civil rights movement.

BOSTON'S FAMOUS NEIGHBORS

Boston's neighbors, Lexington and Concord, were a prominent part of the American Revolution. They were sites of important events and many fascinating historic sites still remain today.

LEXINGTON

A bronze statue of a Minuteman stands at the end of Lexington's main street in front of Battle Green. Battle Green is the site of the first encounter in 1775 between a small group of farmers and Thomas Gage's Redcoats which was the beginning of the American Revolution. Facing the Green is the Brickman Tavern, built in 1690, where the Minutemen gathered before their fateful battle. Across town, British General Percy used the Monroe Tavern, built in 1695, as his headquarters and during the war it served as a hospital for wounded soldiers.

Hancock-Clarke House, one of the oldest museums in the country, stands a few blocks from the Green. This is where Samuel Adams and John Hancock were staying the night Paul Revere and William Dawes rode in to warn of the advancement of the British. This museum has most of its original furniture, which is on display, and an upper bedroom showcases the country's oldest set of bed hangings.

CONCORD

Concord was settled in 1635 and its clapboard and redbrick buildings show its colonial past. A main attraction is the Minuteman National Historic Park with a replica of the Old North Bridge. On this bridge, in 1775, an exchange of musket fire between the Minutemen and the Redcoats became known as "the shot heard around the world."

Concord has many historical homes that belonged to literary giants. Ralph Waldo Emerson owned The Old Manse from 1835 – 1882,which was built by his grandfather in 1770. The Alcott family home from 1858 – 1877, Orchard House, was described in Little Women. Thoreau's solitary cabin at Walden Pond may be toured. Sleepy Hollow Knoll is the burial place of all these literary giants. The Concord Antiquarian Museum houses the contents of Emerson's study as well as having 15 period rooms which are arranged in ascending order from 1680 –1860.

HISTORIC

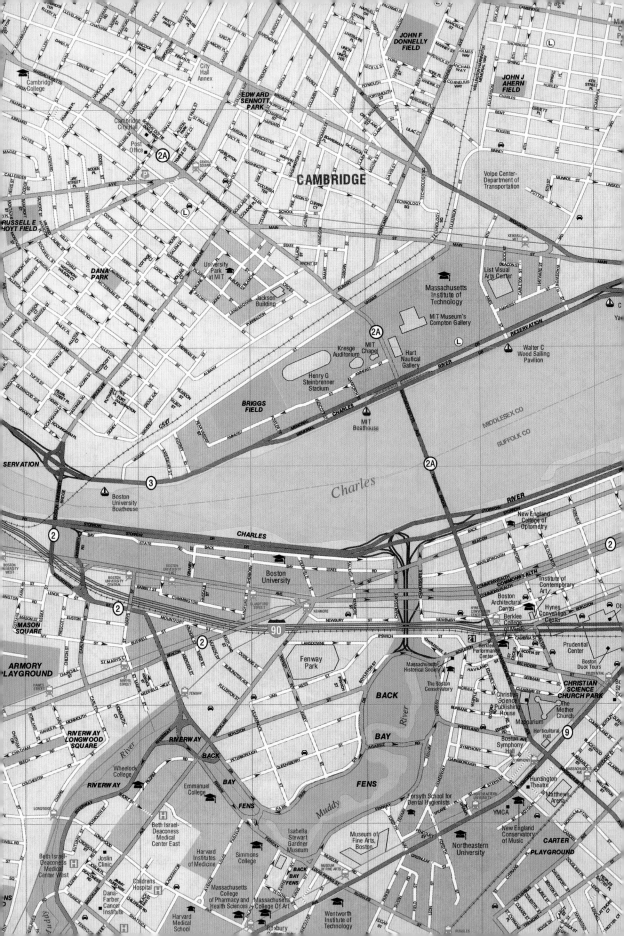

BOSTON COMMON

Boston Common with over 50 acres of green lawns, magnificent trees and serene waterways, is America's oldest public park. Despite the calm atmosphere it has an exciting albeit violent past. In 1634 the land was purchased for a military training site and the British Army used it as a camp during the Revolution. In 1775 they used is as a base from which to launch their assault on the colonial resistance of Lexington and Concord. After the Revolution the townspeople owned and used it as a common pasture for their cattle until 1830. Frog Pond was the place for duels fought by scalawags and gentlemen and also for public hangings. In contrast, it was used for many celebrations and concerts.

PUBLIC GARDEN

FOUNDED
1837

CITY OF BOSTON
DEPARTMENT OF PARKS AND RECREATION
THOMAS M. MENINO   JUSTINE M. LIFF
MAYOR   COMMISSIONER

BOSTON FOUNDED A.D. 1630

NEW STATE HOUSE

The "New" State House, completed in 1798, lies across from the Common. It is the oldest building on Beacon Hill and it serves as the seat of Massachusetts state government, and is regarded as one of the most beautiful and well-situated buildings in the country. The land on which it stands was once John Hancock's cow pasture. The cornerstone of this impressive building that has been used as the model for other state capitols, was laid by Governor Samuel Adams and Paul Revere. The dome is covered in copper with a 23 karat gold finish, a change from its original wood shingles.

JOHN F. KENNEDY LIBRARY AND MUSEUM

The Kennedy Library, designed by architect I. M. Pei, traces the life of John F. Kennedy and the Archives house his personal, congressional and presidential papers. Also part of the Archives are Ernest Hemingway's manuscripts and correspondence.

PARK STREET CHURCH

This Evangelical church with its 217 foot steeple, was the first landmark travelers saw on arriving in Boston. It was founded in 1809 and for 200 years it has been a base for human concerns. In 1818 the first Sunday school opened, in 1824 the first prison aid program began, in 1829 William Lloyd Garrison's first antislavery speech was made here. In 1831 "My Country 'Tis of Thee" was first sung by the church's children's choir.

GRANARY BURYING GROUND

A grain storage building gave its name to the "Granary" and to the Park Street Church site in 1660. Local and state dignitaries, victims of the Boston Massacre and patriots of the Revolutionary-era such as Peter Faneuil, Samuel Adams, John Hancock, Robert Treat and Paul Revere are all buried here.

KING'S CHAPEL AND BURYING GROUND

King James II decreed the establishment of an Anglican parish in Boston in 1688, but was met with the colonists' resistance to sell land for a non-Puritan church. Obeying the orders, the Governor seized a corner of the burial grounds for the Church of England and hired Peter Harrison, America's first architect, to design the church which "would be equal of any in England". Visiting British dignitaries had their own pew reserved for them and before being hanged on the Common, condemned prisoners heard their last sermon here.

FRANKIN STATUE, OLD CITY HALL AND FIRST PUBLIC SCHOOL SITE

Benjamin Franklin's statue outside the Old City Hall is the first of its kind erected in the U.S. The base of the statue shows him as a printer, as a scientist and signing the Declaration of Independence. The nation's oldest public school which Franklin, Samuel Adams and John Hancock attended, is overlooked by his statue. In 1635 the Puritan settlers established the Boston Latin School which is today still operational in Boston's Fenways neighborhood.

In 1865 construction began on the Old City Hall and it served as Boston's City Hall for more than a century. It is made of white Concord granite and has a massive lantern dome. The building has been well preserved and in 1969 the Architectural Heritage Foundation adapted its use as an office building. It is presently occupied by retail and office businesses and serves as headquarters for several Massachusetts preservation organizations.

OLD CORNER BOOKSTORE

The Old Corner Bookstore was originally built by Thomas Crease in 1712 for his residence and apothecary. When the Tichnor and Fields Publishing House occupied the site from 1832-1865, it became known by its name. As a Publishing House it was noted for many famous works such as Walden and the Atlantic Monthly magazine, The Scarlet Letter and others. Longfellow, Oliver Wendell Holmes, Hawthorne and Emerson and other noted authors used the bookstore as a meeting place in the 19th century.

To prevent its demolition, a charitable organization, Historic Boston Incorporated, purchased the building in 1960 and restored the 19th century appearance.

OLD SOUTH MEETING HOUSE

The Old South Meeting House was built in 1729 as a Congregational Church and as it was the largest building in town, it was used for meetings too large for Faneuil Hall. In 1773 over 5000 Bostonians met to discuss the British tea tax, and when Samuel Adams said "This meeting can do nothing more to save the country" at the close of the meeting, is when it became infamous. This led to the "Boston Tea Party" when a group of citizens left the meeting incensed and dumped three shiploads of tea into the harbor. This action forced the closure of the port of Boston by Parliament. The rebellion defining America's history was on the move.

In the 1870's Back Bay became the congregations new location. The Old South Association was formed to preserve the building and association with the paticipation in freedom of speech. It is still active today by sponsoring lectures and exhibits, recreating tea party debates and promoting publications.

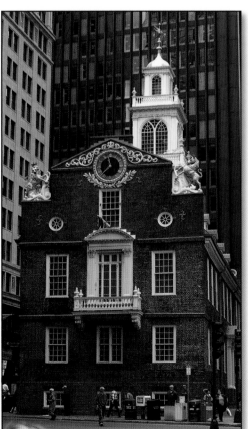

OLD STATE HOUSE AND BOSTON MASSACRE SITE

Before the New State House was built in 1798, the Royal Governor presided over the colonial government from the Old State House built in 1713. The building has a varied history of occurrences including merchant exchanges, heated town meetings, being the site of the Boston Massacre and where the reading of the Declaration of Independence took place from its balcony in 1776. The Bostonian Society now runs a Boston History Museum here, featuring models of ships and colonial artifacts.

The ring of cobblestones in a traffic island in front of the Old State House marks the place of the Boston Massacre. In 1770, tensions were running high between the British soldiers and the colonists and a minor dispute between a wigmaker's apprentice and a British sentry erupted into a violent riot. The relief soldiers aiding the British sentry were assailed by a variety of rocks, snowballs and clubs thrown by the colonists. Five men in the crowd were killed when they were fired upon. The civic leaders, including Samuel Adams, called the event a "massacre" and so it joined the Boston Tea Party on the path to rebellion.

FANEUIL HALL

Peter Faneuil built Faneuil Hall in 1742 and donated it to the city to be used as a meeting and market place. Its second-floor meeting hall was the site of historic and inspiring protests and speeches against the British and iwas called the "Cradle of Liberty" by John Adams. In 1806 Charles Bulfinch enlarged the building to its present size. The lower floor is still a market place and meeting hall and the third floor houses the Ancient and Honorable Artillery Company. When Boston became a city, its use as a government meeting place came to an end. The second floor Great Hall now holds talks by the National Park Rangers.

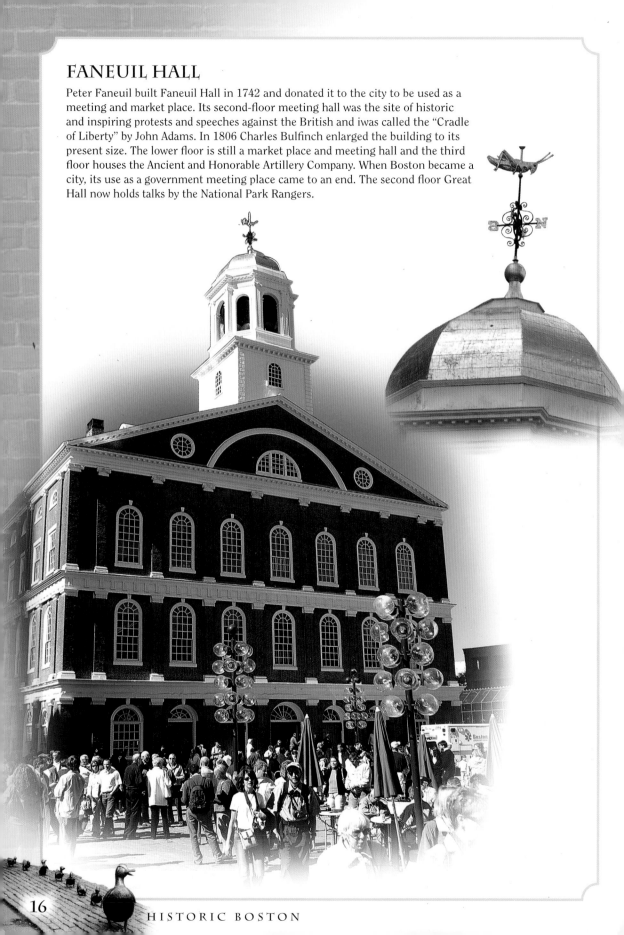

QUINCY MARKET

One of the city's most visited tourist destinations is Quincy Market. Adjacent to Faneuil Hall, Quincy Market with its copper dome, was converted from the wholesale food and distribution center of Boston into a "festival market" in the 1960's. It has a vast number of shops and restaurants with the biggest selection of lobsters anywhere, and street performers are a main attraction.

FENWAY PARK
HOME OF THE RED SOX

GILLETTE STADIUM

In May 2002 the Gillette Stadium in Foxborough, MA opened. This world class facility is the home of the NFL's New England Patriots and the MLS's New England Revolution. The stadium's seating capacity is 68,000 and features a 12 story high lighthouse and a pedestrian bridge.

TD GARDEN
HOME OF THE CELTICS NBA BASKETBALL TEAM AND THE BRUINS NHL HOCKEY TEAM

HOLOCAUST MEMORIAL

In 1995 the New England Holocaust Memorial was dedicated to honor one of the greatest tragedies the world has seen. Situated near Faneuil Hall and other landmarks that stand for freedom and human rights, it gives pause for one to reflect that it stands for the same values. Made of luminous glass, the six towers, representing each of the Nazi death camps, are set on a granite pathway with the name of the death camp inscribed in a dark chamber under each one.

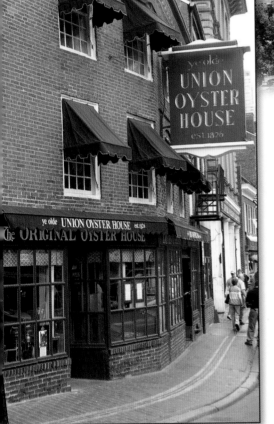

THE UNION OYSTER HOUSE

For more than 250 years the Union Oyster House has been in continuous use and is the oldest restaurant as such in the country. It began life as Capen's Dry Goods Store and when, in 1771, the beginning of the Revolution reached this landmark, was when Isaiah Thomas published the "Massachusetts Spy" from its upper floors. In 1826 it became the Union Oyster House and Tavern.

Over the 250 years of existence it has been used by many and for different reasons. The wives of Quincy, Adams and Hancock sewed and mended clothes here during the Revolution. Boston's young ladies were taught French here by Louis Phillipe in 1796 while he was in exile before he became King of France. A daily occurrence was John Webster imbibing a tall tumbler of brandy and water for each half-dozen oysters he had, usually three dozen. "The Kennedy Booth" in the upstairs dining room was reserved for John F. Kennedy.

BOSTON STONE

The Boston Stone, laid in 1737 in what was supposed to be the exact center of the city, is now fixed to the side of the building at 9 Marshall Street. It was modeled after the "London Stone" marking the center of London, and was later used as a landmark for measuring distances from Boston even though certain cynics thought its site outside a tavern was to attract business. In 1948, the New England Paint, Varnish and Lacquer Association restored it as this artifact was used to grind oil and pigment for making paint.

PAUL REVERE HOUSE

Paul Revere's house, which he owned from 1770 – 1800, is now the oldest house in Boston having been built in 1680. In the thirty years he lived there he made his three most celebrated deeds – his creation of the Boston Massacre engraving, his participation in the Boston Tea party and his famous "midnight ride" to Lexington and Concord. Commercial shops and apartments occupied the house in later years. The histories preservation movement started in 1908 when the Paul Revere Memorial Association restored the building and until today still owns and operates daily tours.

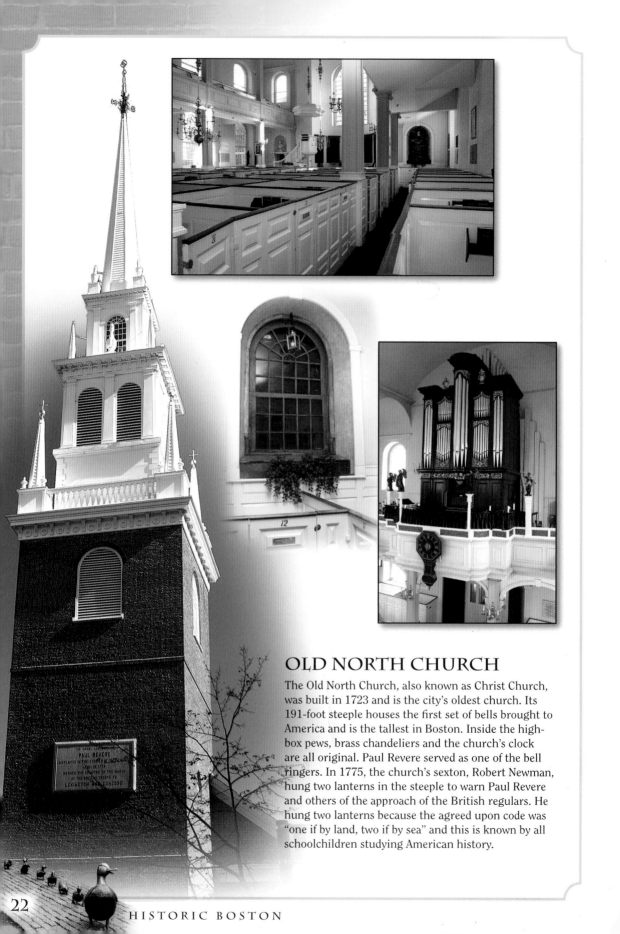

OLD NORTH CHURCH

The Old North Church, also known as Christ Church, was built in 1723 and is the city's oldest church. Its 191-foot steeple houses the first set of bells brought to America and is the tallest in Boston. Inside the high-box pews, brass chandeliers and the church's clock are all original. Paul Revere served as one of the bell ringers. In 1775, the church's sexton, Robert Newman, hung two lanterns in the steeple to warn Paul Revere and others of the approach of the British regulars. He hung two lanterns because the agreed upon code was "one if by land, two if by sea" and this is known by all schoolchildren studying American history.

COPP'S HILL BURYING GROUND

Overlooking the Charles Rivers the Copp's Hill Burying Ground took its name from the family that once owned the land. In 1659 it was founded as

Windmill Hill and the British troops used its elevation as a vantage point from which to fire their cannons on Charlestown during the Battle of Bunker Hill.

The "New Guinea" community of thousands of free blacks, that lived at the base of Copp's Hill, are buried here in unmarked graves. Headstones of the Mather family of ministers, Robert Newman who places the warning lanterns for Paul Revere in the Old North Church's steeple and the founder of the Black Masonic Order, Prince Hall, are all here.

CHARLESTOWN NAVY YARD AND USS CONSTITUTION

Prior to the Battle of Bunker Hill, the British army used the Charlestown Navy Yard, once known as Morton's Point, as a landing base. Being one of the first shipyards in the U.S., hundreds of ships have been built or repaired here and its peak operational period was during World War II when 50,000 people were employed here. An example of the type of ship built here is the USS *Cassin Young,* which is moored at Pier 1. Part of the Boston National Historic Park is 30 acres of the yard preserved by the National Park Service.

"Old Ironsides", the USS *Constitution* is the Yard's most famous resident. She was commissioned by George Washington in 1797. In her long career she never lost a battle, not against the Barbary pirates or the British Army during the 1812 War. Her nickname was coined when during the War of 1812 in a battle with HMS *Guerriere*, her seamen cried "Huzzah! Her sides are made of iron" as cannonballs glanced off her hull. In 1927, using contributions, she was restored and today is the oldest warship afloat. She houses a museum of original artifacts, numerous exhibits, a theatre and gift shop.

Photo taken by Kerri-Ann Tobin aboard Little Miss Magic.

BUNKER HILL MONUMENT

A 221-foot granite obelisk marks the first formal battle of the American Revolution in 1775. The colonial militiamen dug in on Breed's Hill to fortify Charlestown as this site was closer to the water and lower than Bunker Hill where the British were camped. The British soon attacked from their higher point to keep control. To inspire his men and make each shot count, Colonel William Prescott shouted his infamous phrase – "Don't fire until you see the whites of their eyes." The militiamen repelled two major assaults before retreating even though they were out-numbered and out-classed. Before retreating they had killed nearly half of the British soldiers and their bravery encouraged others to continue to fight for independence.

BOSTON'S HISTORIC COLLEGES

Boston has 27 colleges and universities inside its city limits and the surrounding areas have 40 more, educating more than 100,000 students.

HARVARD®

Harvard, established in 1636 across the Charles River in Cambridge, is respected world wide as an outstanding institution of learning. Eight signatories of the Declaration of Independence and six presidents were educated here. Its faculty is made up of many distinguished Americans among whom are more than 20 Pulitzer Prize winners and 27 Nobel laureates.

Harvard is different in that its "campus" is actually Harvard Square, which is a colorful meeting place with coffee shops, boutiques, book stores and sidewalk performers. During the Revolutionary War two of its buildings, Massachusetts Hall and Holden Chapel, were used to house troops. The newer buildings join the 18th and 19th century original ones and have thus spread the university.

MASSACHUSETTS INSTITUTE OF TECHNOLOGY™ (MIT)

Famed MIT in Cambridge was planned as a school of practical science when it was built just after the Civil War. Today it is one of the world's renowned schools of electronics, nuclear and space research with a distinct emphasis on ecological preservation.

BOSTON UNIVERSITY

Boston University is one of the largest independent universities in the country and has students from 135 foreign countries and all 50 states and they number more than 30,000. It is located adjacent to the Back Bay district on the banks of the Charles River.

BOSTON COLLEGE

Boson College is one of the oldest Jesuit, Catholic universities in America. Founded in 1863, it is situated 6 miles from downtown Boston. It has a 116 acre campus and has well over 9,000 undergraduate students and approximately 5,000 graduate students. Pictured is the John J. Burns Library.

NORTHEASTERN UNIVERSITY

Originally this was a part-time night school when it was founded in 1898, but is has grown to encompass more than 66 acres along Huntington Avenue which is also known as the Avenue of the Arts.

BACK BAY/NEWBURY STREET
SHOPPING DISTRICT

The Back Bay area of Boston was originally marshland that was filled-in in the 1800's to expand the city for the settlers. Newbury Street is the shopping area with its stores, galleries, coffee shops and restaurants housed on many different building levels making an expedition to this area very exciting.

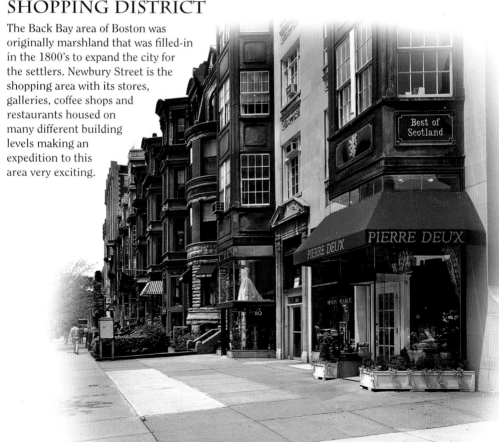

BEACON HILL

Beacon Hill, originally called Shawmut, was first settled by William Blackstone on 50 acres of land of which he kept 6 acres and the balance was sold to the Puritan settlers. It became one of the most prestigious areas of the city and the critic, Can Wyck Brooks wrote of the area's culture that "there were cooks on the slope of Beacon Hill while wolves still howled on the summit." The Puritan settlers objected to Blackstone's carousing with Indians, riding his tame bull at night and imbibing strong liquor. Beacon Hill was named according to a General Court edict that said "There shall be forthwith a Beacon set on the sentry hill at Boston, to give notice to the country of any danger."

The growth in the area began in the 1800's when developers came in and built homes in the Federal, Greek revival and Victorian styles. These homes are built along narrow cobblestone streets. Many notable Americans lived here, among them Henry James and Louisa May Alcott. Beacon Hill was an integral part of the Black American changes of the time. The Underground Railroad used the area extensively. The Black Heritage Trail, which focused on the social, educational and political aspects, linked the Boston African American National Historic site comprising 15 pre-Civil War structures. In 1805, the African Meeting House – the oldest Black church – was formed and served the free Black community as a place of worship and meeting place.

BOSTON PUBLIC LIBRARY

The oldest lending library in the country, the Boston Public Library was founded in 1848 and is situated on the south side of Copley Square. It was part of the plan of bringing cultural and scientific institutions to Boston. It was designed by the New York firm of Mead, McKim and White and took from 1888-1892 to complete. This building that has its walls covered in murals by Sargent, de Chavanees and Abbey, its entryway decorated with sculptures by Pratt and Saint-Gaudens, was meant to be "a palace for the people and dedicated to the advancement of learning."

TRINITY CHURCH

This Episcopalian Church, completed in 1877 and designed by H.H. Richardson, is rated as Boston's most beautiful building, and even though it is surrounded by other imposing structures, it has about 100,00 visitors a year. It is built in the "Richardson Romanesque" style and the interior was designed by La Farge. It has magnificent stained glass windows and dramatic murals. Richardson matched the fresh style of its Rector, Phillips Brooks, for inspiration in the style of the tripartite "Christ in Majesty" windows.

COPLEY SQUARE

Copley Square is surrounded by several wonderful buildings - Boston's Public Library, Trinity Church, Hancock Tower, Copley Place and the Prudential Center. Local residents, business workers from the neighborhood and thousands of international visitors congregate here with the multi-level shopping complex of Copley Square, hotels, offices and condominiums. Copley Square, named after John Singleton Copley, Boston's well known artist in 1883, was originally named Art Square.

FIRST CHURCH OF CHRIST SCIENTIST

This church was established by Mary Baker Eddy, founder of the Christian Science movement, and it serves as the World Headquarters of the Christian Science Church and is known as the "Mother Church." It was constructed from 1894-1906 and its design blends a number of architectural concepts such as Corinthian columns, Romanesque, Renaissance and Byzantine styles.. It has a globe-shaped room, called the Mapararium, in which visitors "walk around the world." It also has one of the world's largest pipe organs.

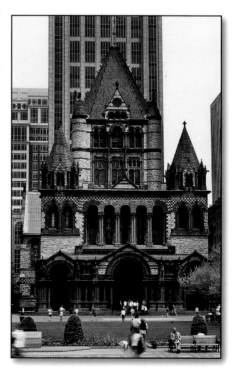

JOHN HANCOCK AND PRUDENTIAL BUILDINGS

Standing 740 feet high, adjacent to Trinity Church, the John Hancock Tower is Boston's tallest building – a blue glass skyscraper. It was designed by I.M. Pei, who also designed the John F. Kennedy Library, and was completed in 1976. Some thought that its proximity to Trinity Church would overwhelm it, but the reflection of the church on the glass makes it seem even larger. The 60th floor of the tower has an observatory with a 360-degree view of the city and on clear days one can see Concord, Lexington and Cape Cod.

The Prudential Building, before the Hancock Tower was built, was one of the tallest in the city having 52 stories. It was completed in 1965 and has 4000 windows and 10 acres of glass walls. The spectacular views of the city can be seen from the Center Sky Walk and markings on the windows help locate the area's well-known landmarks.

LONGFELLOW BRIDGE

The West Boston Bridge, its former name and locally known as the Salt and Pepper Shaker Bridge, was built in 1793. The bridge shortened the distance between Cambridge and Boston as it was now a direct route of three miles instead of the winding eight miles. Later Cambridgeport grew along the roads leading to the bridge.

CHARLES RIVER

The Charles River Reservation has been preserved since 1893 by the Metropolitan District Commission for the use of Boston residents and visitors. It features 17 miles of park and has many recreational facilities such as canoeing, ice skating and in-line skating. The river basin and park was created with the help of the Charles River Dam which controls the water levels. Arthur Fiedler and the Boston Pops had its first performance here in 1929 in the Esplanade Park and summer performances are wide and varied. The Community Boating and Community Rowing are the country's oldest and best public boating programs and thousands have been taught these sports on the Charles River.